Northern Soul

Ron Silliman

Northern Soul

being degree 10 of Universe

Shearsman Books

First published in the United Kingdom in 2014 by
Shearsman Books
50 Westons Hill Drive
Emersons Green
BRISTOL
BS16 7DF

Shearsman Books Ltd Registered Office
30–31 St. James Place, Mangotsfield, Bristol BS16 9JB
(this address not for correspondence)

www.shearsman.com

ISBN 978-1-84861-319-5

ACKNOWLEDGEMENT
A portion of *Northern Soul* appeared as *Wharf Hypothesis*
from Lines chapbooks of Red Hook, NY.
My gratitude to Lynn Behrendt for her support of my work.

Northern Soul

For Barney

Up Quay St
to Deansgate
then over
to Victoria Station,
Northern Rail
West to Liverpool
grey clouds
pillowing the sky
No height
in these fields yet
whatever they're growing
Hedge row as fencing
An older station
at Newton-le-Willows
brick office padlocked
but the chairs on the platform
bright yellow vinyl
then the backsides
of row housing
with thin slivers of yards
School fields
without baseball diamonds
Magpies mistaken
for mockingbirds
Blood pudding
salad
full of rocket
planespotter
in an antiaircraft

unit, learning
first to drive a tank
over the Egyptian desert
then determining
never to leave England again
Sharp shadow over the page
writing into the dark
Notice is hereby given
that it is proposed
to change
the name of Sparrow Park
to Gallipoli Garden
Bury in Bloom
reads the jeep tipped
in aforementioned garden
Fly all the way from London
& what's on the screen
but *Cash Cab*
Squigglies in white paint
at each intersection
mean *Don't park here*
I'm not listening to their conversation
but rather to the language
which I decide must be Greek
understanding not a word
The tall woman is wearing a giant box
plaintively calling your name
The little dog pirouettes
just to see me

The market's a national treasure
but it's just off-brand tack
in vast quantity
United puts away the Arsenal
to reach the final
canals everywhere
Ten percent of the people
own 90% of the land
ergo 90% of the people
live on just ten percent of the land
The streets thus are crowded in the South
Locals discern a course tongue
Wystan Curnow & Barry Schwabsky
in the very same room
Asparagus ravioli
Fleet Street being shorter
than I'd imagined
Cutting short Artie Gold
vomiting between sets
as the turntablist samples
Willie the Shake
photo shoot by the Roman fort
speed at which
towns blur by
feeling blurby — Simon
mit Garfunkel, always
with the cooked tomato
My kingdom for a floss
Trees shimmer perfectly still

but upside down
mirrored by the river
no more than a stream
peat bog in the pine barrens
dogwood's blossoms all but gone
Birds won't fly
in a straight line
The tea, being hot
steamed his glasses
which then cleared slowly
The argument over bitterns
turned bitter — "POETRY
HAS BEEN BURY, BURY
GOOD TO ME"
who has proven
but a meager steward
In the dark but
with the window open
attempting to sort
the symphony of birds
Conch shell mounted
atop a copper spike
Where I come from
fog never foretells rain
but here it is
difficult to discern
where one ends, the other
congeals into drops
First crow at dawn

Maketh one to yawn
The small fort stood
nearly 2,000 years
until amid
the hurly burly of
rapid industrial expansion
it was knocked down
without a second thought
Four trill bird song
or perhaps a female
green-backed heron
The thrill of
the first signature's
binding, white thread
at the margin
is what I first wrote
Wind on the back
of my neck
Soften the
break in the
line, not
as you hear
it, rhetorical
but throated
caught in the
business of
breathing
A kiss that
momentarily

proved a bit
too intense
takes one's —
the choice is in
fact accurate —
breath away
so that it is
oxygen or
the absence thereof
that flushes
the rush of
adrenalin
illuminating the night
Dickens lives
but a block away
Mallard of wood
impaled on a stand
Southernmost tip
of New Jersey
Dear Jimmy,
it's 7:45 AM
in the Woitasek's
beach rental
swans on Lake Lilly
Without much
wind the rain
won't reach me
here below
the balcony

Life understood
as the gradual
expanse of regret
Field guide to
warblers left
on some counter
the day before
Hydrant painted
yellow with
a bright orange top
on an otherwise
county road
Little junco's
big song
mixed with the
tree rodent's bark
Not a squirrel
but a crow
has glided in
to the dead tree
Rain audible
only from tires
rolling over
the river Ex
the river Irwell
all these
nameless canals
The center
of town has

shifted, following
the big hotels
A slow job, bottle
of water in
his right hand
Rain mottles the lake
His biggest failing
is an excess
of earnestness, that
he wants too much
to be liked, not
knowing how
precisely
to ascertain
what is fluid,
instantaneous, flickering
& thus to others
comes across
both as anxious
& eager. The rain
slows, so
you notice the wind
just as vowels
in a diphthong
elongate
until the consonants
that bracket them
begin to hum
A Lhasa Apso

sniffs my calf,
face I see
atop Tibetan demon
portrayals, architect's
model turned into
a doll house, no
right angles
after 354 years,
flowers lean away
from morning wind,
sparrows at the hedge,
heron in flight
renders the invention of arrows
inevitable

        candles
on the glass alas,
sparrows at the hedge
in great quantity,
what I'm after
here is a tone
that is not
the vibration of phonemes
set into motion
but an emotion
at the base of my spine
I will recognize
by virtue of
having once upon a time
been ten years old

so far from this pasture
Tom calls
his septic field
causing Beth to laugh,
Schuyler to turn his head
tho Lulu
shows no reaction
but continues
to chew this
plastic replica
of a clay pot
Thus I spun loose
from any sense of anchor
nor rancor at
the economy of departure
that so propelled
even my ancestors
over oceans
(binocs
buy an ox
bind an
oxymoron)
humid at
ocean's edge
Thunder & lightning
give depth to the sky
Kayaker soup
West End Ave
is in fact

to the East
at least here
in southernmost Delaware
just north
of Fenwick Island
Sweet sad
to awaken
just when the dream's
taken an erotic turn
your friend, without warning,
after all these years
to have opened her robe,
the dress falling
just as you startle awake
The residue of rain
everywhere evident
but the crickets
pulsing in synch
Some conversation
just out of hearing
I can tell gender & tone
but only that
words indistinguishable
but for the act of themselves
Lone sparrow
makes a kissing sound
The traffic
a continual shush
The wind, 11 stories up

not silent but
as tho a flag
or sheet unfurling
Lewis Warsh
at the local market
The tyranny of predicates
My spine in the morning
Even here one
hears voices from
the street
this lamp throws shadows
the way a ventriloquist
a good one
displaces her voice
the puppet muttering
alone in its corner
You can see who's awake
in that highrise condo
just by the lights
but not who's lying there
sleepless, alone
angry or sad, in pain
there in the dark
traffic already constant
at 5 in the morning
Dear Chris, hello
that generation
already slipping away
A fan with a broken blade

Of course there's a story
The only tile
there above the stove
chickpea puree
beside the perfect trout
sprouts roasted
alongside apples
in maple cider
so the first taste is sweet
Cranes in the brain
in the rain
    in the pond
beyond which
a train
silhouettes the horizon
which, when it whistles,
sends these long birds aloft
The pansies are planted
after a harsh winter
Last fall's last leaves
finally raked
Roger across the road
digging in his tiny
hillside garden plot
Up the hill, barely audible
woodpecker's paradiddle
but no leaves yet
or barely any
tho the grey forest

starts to tinge green
just from the buds
not warm yet
but the cusp of warm
Many birds go silent
at the advance of crows
At the high point of
this hill the oldest
barn in Philadelphia
but behind me
on the far side
of the river the loud
whistle of a train
I hear a tractor's
soft distinct growl
the coo of a rock dove
tho these robins
are as fat
as they are
silent, honey bees
plump with spring
O wild ancient house
with hand cut
stone pillars you
wade into garden
then crouch something
yellow something
barely purple butter
fly no larger

than the nail of this finger
Repent! Says the barn
Dreams in which
I come home &
the computer's destroyed
the books are all missing
& no one will explain
The four tunnels
of the Pennsylvania Turnpike
the distance between
rage & sadness
the former but a mask
for the latter
Where the Monongahela
meets the Ohio
red bud trees
at forest's edge
the way cows
when resting
tuck their legs under
Why is Glenn Beck so sad
Books mean nothing
save for what we've read
high sky made low
by misty rain
By river
to the Gulf
& later by train
all the way to Philadelphia

remains of Fort Pitt
the bridges deliberately picturesque
Obscure fact about Pittsburgh
is that here was born
the great failed state
of Czechoslovakia
prsi, prsi
a harvest dance
in a great hall
under 1120 lights
two of which
have burned out
They look like aging bikers
but for the SUV
two kinds of Indians
pause at the restaurant door
I recount the tale
of the day
John & Yoko walked into the store
O lyrical moniker
PNC Park
Maz not Yaz
before that was a term
for birth control
side effects may include stroke
cops are like plaque
it only takes one
to clot the artery
young women cluster

later in the lobby
lives framed
by a cordon of
yellow tape, in
the shower I
notice sirens
louder, closer
than they ought to be
Later, sez Jesse
the coroner's van
outside the old house
of the little woman
nobody ever saw
Oh great canopy
of oaks, maple, poplar
dogwood, crabapple, wild
cherry, I hear
a jet but never look up
The squirrel's trill
nearly a "bird call"
Morning & crows, days
without power
in the middle of summer
water in the birdbath
stale & discolored
A daddy-long-legs bright orange
in the grass, those tiny
purple flowers so much larger
than he (how not

to assign gender)
The laughter next door
of toddlers wild
as the crows you hear
what you fear
or maybe not
not to have learned
the names of flowers
then to sit in the garden
the sound of a basketball
with just a single source
a bird that prefers
to whistle She pulls
the dachshund on his leash
What occurs in the line
is itself prose
tho the line is not
How do I know
what I meant by that
Smidge as unit of
measure, hence meaning
hence morning the great
claw of the once-red
garbage truck snaps
old discarded rear door
right in half, pulling it in
Every squirrel shoots
up to the tree tops
until it passes

the road again quiet
not a year for cicadas
First the birds, then
distant traffic
woodpecker's paradiddle
Last the door
of the garage next door
Gradually friends
are being stripped away
You say "Hi"
as tho it were a question
& speak in whispers
even into the microphone
save occasionally
for a terminal vowel
The vow you made to
forgive your father
At your service
it is he
who bids farewell
knowing absolutely
he has lived too long
The cookie not
as crunchy
as I had imagined
the cheese
grows soft & sweeter
From the photo the
closed-in porch

looked like nothing
but the instant I set foot there
I knew I was happy
tiny puppy, industrial leash
Circular stairs
to a rooftop deck
Sitting up, connecting
the bikini top
A boat in shadows
drifting By then
a breeze had risen
& the shades were longer
That one bird with
the same five-note song
over & over
has stopped What
in the water
makes that kissing sound
Arcs of the gull,
retort of the grackle
Don't know about God
the man laughs
but ghosts exist,
how about that?
What I see in the mirror
she says, is an old woman
with a large scar
His wife grew smaller
every year A wound

where once there'd been
an eye A hand
absent the index finger
It's the small birds I hear
all territorial before dawn
Went to the carpenter
instead of the dentist
so he's hammering boards
into my mouth Two teens
comparing tales of woe,
square pegs on
an unforgiving planet
First AC unit of the day
kicks on across the canal
The reflection of homes shimmer
in this not-quite-still water
What Northern means in the UK
vs, say, in Tuscaloosa
Black-headed gull
settles just for a moment
Right at dawn, the cacophony
quiets down One frog
in all that din
The laughing mallard
Midway through the third signature
with five more to follow
Flags heavy with yesterday's rain
what I had not yet found
was the toaster

It was warm, even
in the shade, even
with the breeze, so
he let the book
rest open on his stomach
as he lay upon the couch
on the deck & slept
A swordless swordfish
hung on the wall
The chopper was blocking
the highway but
nobody seemed to mind
Drivers stood beside their vehicles
sipping from giant plastic mugs
In the distance an airplane
pulled a banner too faded
to read Two women
waddled into Candy Kitchen
Courtly, debonair, a prince:
Puss-in-Boots
Large vinyl porpoise
holding the mailbox
Dozens, hundreds
of jellyfish
just below the water's surface
Crabs' claws a deep blue
Out over the marsh
an eagle sails by
holding a large white fish

Words evaporate
before I reach this pen
line as flat
as this lake's horizon
Tea delivered
in a one-cup pot
in a high-ridged saucer
which is itself
a kind of pond
Man on a cellphone says
"If only I
could get my
ears to pop"
Taxis spout rooftop signage
Cyclists wear neon yellow
lives in parallel
heading south
Backpack hiding
in the chair in
plain sight
Every 30 minutes
the news of Spain
the ball rolls right
up the striker's
back   women cry
a quick scene of snow
some Gaudí tower
for a backdrop
Imagine say the Eastern

US seaboard each
state a new tongue
while upstairs
dancers twist a slow
Westcoast swing
to the Harlem Blues Project
some house band
on Bleecker
his rich baritone her
leg wrapped completely
around that of
her partner he
mostly strikes poses
it's all in her hips
downstairs Lorca
imagines New York
squid, mussels, peas
mixed over rice
These tall brick
buildings bring
the sky in
close   Kiefer's
white dress
filled with shards
of thick glass
Helicopters
out over the Hudson
clouds drifting
almost as fast

On a chair
at the dance floor's side
she adjusts her hose
until everyone
stands transfixed by
her black panties
First TV
visible thru a window
later whole blocks
of lit apartments
entirely without people
We come out of the tunnel
into a different world
clouds all but invisible
but for the way light
gathers at the horizon
but for the way
light gathers
Everyone this year
tucking tight jeans
into their boots
Distinguishing Missouri
from Arkansas up
in the air without
 any benefit of rivers
Light scrim of cloud
translucent far below
"Fire in the hole"
shouted out in each

direction   best then
not to be a hole
A*hole understood
euphim... You
phim whatever that is
you fam... We
are. Family.
Your brother & your sisters
& me. Nods off
with his Nook standing upright
tray open, not in the locked
upright position. Mid-
day midweek, 13
laptops turned on
in the cabin, 5 watching
movies (I don't
recognize a one), two
playing games, all but
one of the rest
doing email. What
you look like as I pass,
head tilted back,
eyes shut, mouth
open. Painting
of a crowd scene
in the forest   Each
bit has three
distinct phases:
the hardened outer

shell that he
thinks of generically
as "candy,"
sugar made brittle
which tends to
crack or bursts
under the pressure of
incisors, a meaty
almost soft
chocolaty layer,
the sudden presence of
whose taste
triggers recognition
before you even
notice how badly
the milk betrays
the milk chocolate
& you reach, a-
symmetrical as any
miracle, a crisp
almond core
Such a thing as
anesthesia school
I hear the shuffling
of a deck of cards
By habit, stick out
a pair of fingers
around which
to wrap the other

hand, the pair
resting in my lap
Red sky at
morning softens
immediately into
oranges & yellows
high over Sebastopol
City no taller than
its trees when
the yellows dominate
it's time to
wait for the sun
next thought, instanter
the hubris of Main St
come to Nassau Ave
Meditating under a loud clock
souvenir chocolate
Bulldog looks up one
interprets the expressions
as if human
but your own seem
no less transparent
or opaque tries
to remember the intensity
of "casual" sex
young woman barefoot
in a hotel corridor
then five more
in identical slippers

herd effect

flarf-like

Besses o' th' Barn

short proses

an absence of electronics

impoverishes the pocket

shaving his head

bares the moles & lumps

There is something nostalgic

to all this newsness,

yet another poet

scribing answers to

Sunset Debris

He leans forward

to give Stephen a kiss

footsteps at dawn

here on the fifth floor

We know they don't

have earthquakes

or at least don't expect them

from the presence of

brick ceilings

Died it says here

of a blood clot

singing barefoot

in Huthian

you could look it up

Traveling with an old man's bladder

in a young man's sun

Pulls her close
to gain a kiss
not noticing
how her back
arches & stiffens
Chef doesn't do nasties
Homage
to Jonathan Wms
is lunch in the "jardin"
at the Ram's Head
in Disley
topped w/ Yorkshire Pudding
You are the dues
I have to pay
Particulars vibrate
with their own recognition
Catherine's bouquet
upon a white pillow
and a border of
red poppies
looking as one might
expect three days later
not so many yards from
the tomb of
Geoffrey Chaucer
Is the wheel turning?
Quotation is its own remorse
Gap between
the story you give

& the one you
want to (be)li(e)ve
Between orchard & a torture e-
nunciate the distinction
Sour cream pretzels
more startling
than these words
Sinks don't soak books,
sloppy splashing
inattentive
individuals — a small
bunny not
much bigger than
a squirrel
Young man
suffering dwarfism
drags a red wagon
delivering papers
wrapped in
light blue plastic
A young woman with
a huge white dog
Tree with its top
all gone
just above the burl
(recently enough
the wood underneath
still looks raw
lines, loons, looms

limes, limbs
Sirens in great quantity
A goldfinch on the burl
of the truncated oak
A pale green moss
When the sirens
stop close
I'm reminded
of the hospital's
proximity
albeit unseen
The car rolling
slowly up the alley
Grand old home
turned to apart-
ments, ornate
hand-carved bannisters
beside the linoleum stairs
 "What means it
'Screwed the pooch'?"
A stack of cushions
beside the wicker chairs
All this dust
in Black Rock City
A watched microwave
A trio of bicyclists
in identical helmets
The broken tree

cut back to a stump
Parallel stairways,
one from entrance hall
wide & direct,
the other narrower
with less light
turning midway
from next to the kitchen
New generation
of boxy sedans
nobody wants
another Boomer president
Crossing that T
when we come to it
Not so much a balcony
as a second-floor porch
Spends all night
trying to get
her blood sugar down
Nobody gets
(me least of all)
   the secrets
     of the linebreak
In this climate
to have no indoor parking
means some serious
digging out
Names the dog
Dog Names

the dog Cricket
Red fox, dead fox
3rd storey
brick opera house
right by Keuka Lake
Add blackbirds to the mix
Mottled sky
a B&B
right next to the school
not so bad in summer
North Sacramento 1958
Dragonflies hover
over home plate
gorgeous & menacing
& harmless
It is against the law
to own moon dust
& this was
little more than smudges
on adhesive tape
The decades I've traveled
just to deploy
that word in a poem
A case full
of stuffed birds
plus one
white weasel
as an ornament
to the room,

the wallpaper black
but for the sprigs
of impossible fruit
blueberries & peaches
on the same line
Hawk's wingspan is flat
that of the vulture
more of a V
high over the creek
east of Montour Falls
Historical markers
the length of
Sullivan's March
Bright Blue Sign
commemorates Camptown
Races sing this song
doo dah D
Judith Day a long
ways from our days
at the 'Tute
fruit of the narrative
ripe as a bing
cherry Imagine
pits as a mode
of divination
whose motive
we assign as benign
if unknowable
Old green barn roof

barely visible over
wild summer brambles
female fox
aggressively defends
new brood, I try
to fathom
what makes a line
Cricket stays invisible
albeit loud
in that small clay pot
Ghost's name
is Millianne
not to be
confused with
that nervous gentleman
who hovers about the
basement Big rig
filled with flattened cars
held on with
some kind of netting
Man with a migraine
What one sees
the world as it was
early 21st Century
(as I was raised
by those born in the 19th)
Picket fence porch border
every second post removed
Little flatbed trailer

holds a lawn tractor
Tricycle construction
simple, a wire frame
atop flat board base
a hitch, a pair of wheels
I rise at 5, write
then return to bed
Morning dreams
so often erotic
all I remember
is waking aroused
That jogger
with a limp
Taxicabs
slowly circling
the cluster of hotels
looking for dawn
flights to the airport
A breeze discernible
on the back of
my neck Sue
Domain whose name
I've heard for decades
as Pseudo
Main   Planes
out of Reagan
low enough here
to appear a straight line
Don't Dump

stenciled on sewer's
curbside cover
Chesapeake Bay Drainage
Sound of geese
but no geese in sight
Ten black limos
in a line
Each hotel rooftop
with its
electronic bric-a-brac
How many decades
have I waited
to write
with its
as a line?
Someone distant is shouting,
anger in his voice
Giant truck:
US Food Service
Brand new light poles
designed to look quaint
A grill in the walk
all along the stone wall
intended to
drain away rainwater
By the dawn light
high on the side
of that tall cloud,
I discern I

must be facing south
I never sleep
10 hours I seldom
sleep 6
until of course I do
eleven if you count
the show I
thought I was watching
At next table
couple speaks rapidly
in some version
of Chinese
young gal very
professional in a
bright red suit
bouncing from
table to table
explaining menus tran
slating for six
tables at least
sound system soft
reggae First
closed-up swimming
pool I see
this year
Angry carbs
wheat toast is thick
Why serve hash browns
for breakfast

More Chinese couples arrive
mostly women
young gal bouncing about
has I see a printout
names & faces
$15 hotel breakfast
worth maybe half that
Willie Nelson singing
Poncho & Lefty
usted está aquí
it's not the gun shops
nor the pawn shops
up in these little
mountain towns
but the gun-&-pawn
shops together
the woman at
the gas station
sayin' "Do you know
how far
it is to Tennessee?"
Mountain wasps
up in the rafters
sluggish, not
bothering no one
The family she
grew up with
entirely gone
Not one inch

of dry wall
in the entire house
Lamp throws shadows
as well as light
the next page
looms
hard over these words
Page 43
you will read
differently if
there are 94 to the book
than if there are just
45, What about
523 what then
little hen
Don't let that
curdle your cream
Outside, two creeks
are audible, strong
tho only one can be seen
up here, first light
shaping the sky
makes you wonder
what precisely
is or was
a Caney Fork
Toe restlessly investigates
contours of its shoe
but the mind

passing fixates
instead on that
lovely binding of vowels
together *OU* how
it reshapes the mouth
there it is again —
even as it's not
spoken aloud
my new
baseball cap
has its
distinct smell
Eddie's mom
born in that house
with the green roof
right there by the road
mountain folk
who turn out to be kin
by virtue of marriage
to the gal who
oversaw the construction
of the new church
Now a light
over the next hill
coffee pot
with a mind of its own
clapper on the wind
chime sways
without hitting

any of the tongs
Trestle in the park
leading nowhere
Where in the room
one hears the plucked
violin (wanting
to tell
the bow from the body)
The soprano silent
on a sideways stool
At the Planck length
data is not lost
perhaps
the way the uncredited drummer
on the one-hit wonder's
one hit
slides the brush
over the cymbals
or the lone attendant
straps herself in backwards
facing the cabin
puddle jump
to Canadian capitol
delayed when someone
steals the pilot's bags
as if
as ifness itself
had a self
second in line

for take off
the opposite of province
sun trapped
in a gap in
the clouds
the view over Belle Isle
then suddenly the sky
Francophone Vietnamese
hostess offers chopstick,
hence ethnic Chinese
Beautiful city
if you like winter
"Watch for falling ice"
the bridge to Quebec
& back, a bit
bedraggled by travel
white chocolate
raspberry truffle ice cream
in each room
multiple images of tulips
tugboat whistle
on the Rideau Canal
makes me long for the Moika
long ago
            like the vast
canyon of computers
here at the CBC
or the overpriced
but quite decent

salmon served
skinside up
atop some veggies
too thoroughly cooked
we walked back
in a swirl of snow
bad rhythms
smoothed over
by the heating fan
the cabbie's Hindi
with an Eritrean tone
Head scarves on Bank Street
One embassy (Nigeria)
going for the armed bunker look
while catty-corner / Hungary
opts for a stately
mansion
new snow for old
large gold balls of falafel
A beautiful woman
in intense pain
from a concussion
months later
the band plays
with its back to
the bar window
Atomic Rooster
try to
unpack that

                    Instant
of panic
Have I lost this book?
but it's under
a stack in the backpack
turned in fact sideways
Picnic in a brownfield
what used to be
Water Street in Ypsi
Barrett cites
each closed fab plant
as we pass
                    Who
in the dream
am I kissing
& why here
where the old mountain mall
has been reduced
to rubble to
make room for a new
mountain mall all
tractors & chain link
then she steps back
becoming immediately naked
then just as rapidly
disappears altogether
Giant pitcher of mango juice
two kinds of corn
(one baby, the other

as orange as
that pepper)
Lets go
he says, leading
right to the
middle of
an unbroken wall
the cane in
his backpack
folds into sections
Warm air
blasts through the vents
Is that a
true
constituent?
Woman right next to her
one of my
wife's better friends
now equally naked
(as if I'm to choose)
but equally gone
tho never have I been
to a mountain mall
this rubble stays rubble
I shut my eyes
but tears won't come
Warmth of the lamp
by the side of my face
Black squirrel

is in fact

Melanistic Eastern Grey

Impulse to

resort to hitching

At the

Tim

Horton's a

half

dozen seniors

while away the day

Tattoo peeks

from shoulder of blouse

Mosque in basement

where they keep

the freezers

Flowers jut yellow

from her bun

Watch cap

on a hot day

Nameless harmony

café music

this one with dark glasses

pushed back like a hair clip

"Felice,

ham & cheese"

says the counter guy

making it rhyme

Tall gal

with a narrow waist

I hear him mixing
in a plastic bowl
Under all these voices
a single mandolin
the small dark balls
atop the dried carrots
are roast duck hearts
Persimmon salad
with watercress
& thinner-than-paper
sliced radish
A hotel in
one's own city
Earlier I'm dragging
barrels of wood chips
out to the paths
thru the trees
old wild cherry
burl-covered
cut flat maybe ten feet up
what the straight line
says to the forest
Dawn above
the glass dome
at Wharton
One dreams the letter
before one writes it
architects it
in the midst of other

activities
plays phrases over
in the mind, in
the gym, standing
in the woods
squirrel's tail
at one foot of the tree
& only then
begin to write
Just for the halibut
Low fog
on Walnut Street
The Russian
Bangladeshi gal with
a thing about
Spain
      Try
reading words with-
out being sucked
into each one's
context
Hear that con-
Still, 52 years hence
the only
World Series game ever
in which nobody
ever struck out
Each page
being one page closer

The freeway close
but not visible
from this bench
hotel day staff
cruising in
What percentage
of engines
individuate
like that coughing Harley
Birds reiterate
their call for dawn
& that way
must be East,
night failing first
along that horizon
Your voice
clear as a
in the next room
2 AM
yet when I rise
to see what's going on
you're sound asleep
Music in the hotel
lobby 5 AM
excessively perky
Night staff, sleep deprived
appear exhausted
are silent
Back in my room

everything's still dark
Old high-back easy chair
in a familiar room
in Oakland
having seen pelicans
first thing
limited number
of pages remaining
the one tatt
I can make out
reads USMC
tho I recognize
that rolled-up
faux parchment souvenir
Declaration of Independence
leaps up
to help that woman
raise her suitcase
up into
the overhead bin
You can't use e-readers
during take-off
the Coliseum lit up
= the A's are in town
Baggy black pants,
rhinestone skulls
on each of the back pockets
Long straight off-blond
hair dyed

now blue, blue-green
Black leather porkpie hat
Train rises up
from the tunnel
everyone reaching
for their cellphone
the trains more frequent
than I remember
My grandmother born right there
115 years
this next September
Valencia feels intense
smell of weed
outdoor café
I realize
they've changed
the crosswalks
knowing it's raining
or has rained
by the sound
Tall man with large skull rings
carries a harp
White woman
says to a black child
"You listen
to your mother"
You could count
the languages
just walking

down this street
with your eyes shut
& if you were good
you could discern
the varieties of Spanish
Less than one
hour at the
coffeehouse &
we become aware
of the older guy
with the black dyed
Beatles wig who
either must be
a narc or
small time dealer
Fresh perfectly
cooked salmon
under a bland
tapenade atop
a bed of
chopped (al-
beit from a can)
beets,
      tho
the escargots were
perfect
      parking &
reparking
the car in

my sleep
      Trying
as I drive
to i.d. the hawk
as it swoops low,
three horizontal stripes
atop its tail
the Grateful Bagel
with just possibly
the least
expensive espresso
anywhere in the nation
light atop the page
too bright
All these arty
notebooks so
poorly designed
pens expensive
but without heft
Young man
outside chain
coffee house sings
Black girl, black girl
thinking it
a Kurt Cobain tune
sign on
the marquee
of the Oaks
Theatre reads

Available
but still
across from
the Albany Bowl &
just down the
street the
Hotsy-Totsy Club
carries on
Football helmet
on the lawn of
the house in
which I
grew up
is deep blue
the grass unkempt
that corner I think of
as Hinks
Lily at
28 is
gorgeous
her mother
no less so
Hoppy Poppy IPA
L & her
migraines
Denny dead
within 3 months
of retirement
point at which

what visit
will be my last
to survive is
to sneak past
all the traps
Stones in
my head sing
This may be
the last
prime the pump
as if this
ink were blood
3 count line
like a horse
with a limp
What then?
Stingray flaps
against the wooden pier
as she reaches for a towel
to cover its barb
Lone whimbrel at water's edge
Pelican rises up
slowly from the surf
but what I'm noticing
back to the setting sun
are those mountains
snow-capped
east of LA
Drive time

"Happy Talk"

        chatter

just below audible

in hotel elevator

Dip the baguette

in black bean soup

"No' yet"

he replies when

I ask

if he's caught anything

from the Seal Beach pier

that missing first 't'

Mexican accent

Her smart phone

matches the tank top

A rabbit in

the chaparral

by the book store

Black-n-white tennies

with bright

yellow laces

Gauge each passerby

by the number

& kind of

bags they carry

Pacing as he

talks on the phone

cigarette in his other hand

as he scratches his hair

tip of the ash

toppling in

She holds

one arm

away from her body

to balance

the bags she

lets hang

from the opposite shoulder

A new ink cartridge

means a new idea

each letter's line

suddenly lush

two days devoted

to rereading

my earliest texts

each carton

so lovingly (is

that not

the word?) carefully

filed, each

file labeled in pencil

endless sunwashed patios

of the Student Union

Glass display of

giant horned beetles

What the ear allows

the eye makes out

tall cone of

shrimp, beans
in some kind of
tempura, plus
calamari lightly cooked
but without
tentacles (the tastiest
part!) in the dream John
Granger in
the body of
Jed Rasula says
to me "you
have a lot
of decisions to make"
Ranger says
of the Border Patrol
"They don't own this
preserve," Mexico
on the next ridge, "they
just act like they do"
gulls in one
cluster, ducks
in another
lone bufflehead
on the far side, 3
cormorants atop
a small dead tree
rising up from the pond,
helicopters low & loud
over the campus

each page heavier to turn
than the last, she
sent in her place
three lovers to the reading
with the instruction that
they should talk about her
but they were so
circumspect, bemused
& polite, we
38 years later
pause to consider
just whom we might send &
what they might say
daylight emerges as I write
sun-washed sky
hummingbirds by
the half dozen
Neighbor's truck
powering up
tho the train is crowded
the man in the stained
yellow suit
grey felt trilby
that he wears backwards
sings a damaged
version of *Rawhide*
Outside, on the road,
traffic is stopped
for miles

               Tyrion
Lannister
stares down from a billboard
an ad for an app
Fog occludes
Chicago skyline
Older, heavier
no longer a boy
the unmistakable voice
of Ilya Kutik
succotash atop
the slightest bed
of pasta, a few
sprouts just
for the texture
atop which
skin side up
two small filets
of trout
               I try
not to rush
the reading
A long day
of Russians
Such light as one finds
at 5:30 in the morning
What you can tell
about this day's sky
is only that

the fog is not
so low as to
obliterate
the tops of buildings
Data more raw than this fish
that only I can interpret
tho only when sleeping
yet we're parking, leaving
all this sushi behind
something makes me
want to cry
took the cypress
back to his studio
where it was cut
into sections from which
molds were made
that were then sent
to Japan, where a studio
of master woodworkers
specializing in
temple restoration
were then employed
to replicate it exactly
in a new block of cypress
to stand in museums
the way he'd found it
fallen in the woods
I meant to say words
as I heard them

before I arose
as if this were
what I'd done with my life
            Pre-
cisely
            as tho the Stones
the very early Stones
were singing *This may be*
the last page, may
be the last
page I don't know
tho it's not
            Day's first
siren mingles
with the sounds of a jet
each vibrating
through this echoey
urban canyon, the bark
somewhere in the distance
of a small dog, attempting
to sort through
last night's dinner
by the taste(s) in my mouth
Hotel showers on
distant floors
echo overhead
sign on the
backside
of the small

brick cinema
Geneva, NY
where the title
should be
left blank
          Bubble
of ink on
the pen's tip
streaks my finger
tip when I
brush it off
Letters I write
vs. those I print
even in the same word
(as if
words ever
were the same)
Lake's surface never still
each page turning
rushes toward conclusion
my body also
alien vessel that it is
Half moon translucent
in the morning sky
finches play tag
in small lake-front park
Radio & TV mingle
in hotel restaurant air
At the café

a priest is reading
Yves Bonnefoy
in Italian
Young gal in a tank top
obviously lifts weights
50 diners at
the outdoor café
holding 75 conversations
                    Bookseller
asleep in his stall
in the sun
One black ink
more pale than the other
First sounds before dawn
up from the plaza:
someone is attempting
unsuccessfully
to kick start their scooter
gulls laugh
high over Travestere.
someone is stacking
empty milk crates
onto a dolly, one talking
his baritone gruff
but the language
something I don't understand
(not African, not
"Western")
                    delivery

trucks
outnumber Smart Cars
someone is repeatedly coughing
Ahoy Koi
My elbow, my knee, my shelf
stomach loud
with the decision last night
to rise up
from the bed
metal plate
right next to the street lamp
that when you drive over it
makes a noise
inaudible (like the cooing
of pigeons) until
you notice it just once
(like dollies
hauling milk crates)
Roar of metal awnings
storage for small shops
but for the one
that's a book stall
beside which each night
two women bed down
homeless but not
without domestic order
blankets atop sleeping
bags atop
large sheets of cardboard

this pen which
is over 30 years old
may not make it to 40
What then?
                    Another
panini for
Mother Cabrini
or echoes
not so much in
the head as
of it
            Michelangelo's brain
there on the ceiling
A flock of French
school girls in
close quarters on
a hot day
All the sexual
one's-up-man-ship
of 14-year-olds
At the next table
a woman is buying
3 silk shawls
from the vendor who
has interrupted their
descent   A string
of carabinieri
roar down the cobbled
street

In paintings
of this
period porpoises
appear toothsome
& fierce
The accordionist
wanders down the
plaza playing
Roll out the
barrel, we'll
have a barrel
of fun her hand
slips down
from the small
of his
back to
pat him on the ass   I
hear the horse
before I see it
At Termini
the tagging
on the outskirts
of the station, on
the trains themselves
is more classic, more
legible than
in the US
poppies grow wild
beside the tracks

Prosody of Italian
Old Waterman Pen
lapsing into blue
conductor mimes
 Irwin Corey
A continent south
of Deansgate
my turn as Dr Who
Old wanderer
When you moan When
owl-wise by hindsight
the laughing monk
blue stone of the road
here in the Roman Forum
hoopoes & honey buzzards
this tree for olives
that one for figs
Tuscans build walls
where Umbrians just don't
First rooster, best
moon translucent
high over Umbertide
nightingales & cuckoos
no syllable left untouched
fog drifts over the valley
what time have I left
to live in this dream?